How to Flirt With Women

Easy Conversation and Texting Techniques to Spark Interest, Make Her Laugh, and Get Her Chasing You

Cole McBride

losses, direct or indirect, that are incurred as a result of the use of the information contained within this document, including, but not limited to, errors, omissions, or inaccuracies.

Table of Contents

INTRODUCTION.. 1

WHERE YOU MIGHT HAVE GONE WRONG.. 1

CHAPTER 1: WHAT WOMEN WANT 7

UNDERSTANDING THE FEMALE PERSPECTIVE.................................... 7
Key Notes From the Chapter on What Women Want...... 12

CHAPTER 2: LISTENING TO HER BODY LANGUAGE 15

A WOMAN'S BODILY CUES 15
Key Notes From the Chapter on Listening to Her Body
Language 22

CHAPTER 3: HUMOR FEEDS THE SOUL 25

WHY LAUGHTER IS THE BEST MEDICINE.. 25
Key Notes From the Chapter on Humor Feeds the Soul... 31

CHAPTER 4: MASCULINITY... 35

HOW TO BECOME MORE SELF-AWARE.. 35
Key Notes From the Chapter on Masculinity 43

CHAPTER 5: JUST BE YOURSELF 47

WHY ACTING NATURAL IS BENEFICIAL.. 47
Key Notes From the Chapter on Just Be Yourself 53

CHAPTER 6: COMMUNICATION IS KEY 57

WHY BROKEN COMMUNICATION IS AT THE ROOT OF FAILURE............ 57
Key Notes From the Chapter on Communication............. 64

CONCLUSION... 69

HOW TO GET THE GIRL CHASING YOU 69

REFERENCES 75

Introduction

Where You Might Have Gone Wrong

*When all things go bad, do not think so badly about all things,
instead think about the things that made all things bad and
change something!* –Ernest Agyemang Yeboah

If you ever navigate into avenues untried, you are
bound to find a few bumps in the road. Many things
between men and women can go wrong due to a lack of
understanding and good communication. Knowing
what not to do in interactions with women will guide
you on how to correctly address them and treat them in
an appropriate manner. The aim is always to learn from
your mistakes and find ways to improve.

Imagine that you and one of your friends are at a bar
and have seen a group of beautiful women lounging in
a dark corner. You make eye contact with your
wingman of the night and indicate with a nod of your
head in the direction of the group of women. Having
done this before, your friend is familiar with your
signals and nonverbal cues. Both of you ease away from
the bar area where you were seated and make your way
over. However, as you approach, the women lose their

smiles and give you an unwelcome look. I am sure we have all experienced this kind of confidence-crushing brush-off.

Dating can be quite hard for lots of men as approaching women has become increasingly difficult. It is no longer the 1950s and women certainly do not act like the women of those days. No longer are women docile, all sweet smiles and mum. These days, approaching certain women can be like going toe-to-toe with one of the bros! Women today do not look at men with doe eyes or as if they are some type of superhuman specimen. Frankly, many of us have not lived up to that ideal either.

Constantly getting the brush-off from women can cause us to have some doubts. The blows to one's ego and confidence can be devastating as ill confidence in one area can affect us in many different areas. I guess that is one lesson we can learn from such encounters; to not let our inflated sense of self guide us. Women sincerely detest egotistical men! Being full of yourself can be a major turn-off. When approaching a woman, one should balance displaying confidence and humility.

Embarrassing situations such as getting rejected can play around in our heads for days, messing with our confidence, and this experience may have us shying away from women for a while. One too many of these occurrences may have even turned some of us nasty or bitter. Certain jerks have made it difficult for us when we approach women because a woman might have had negative experiences that made her believe that all men are alike. These jerks often lash out at women after being rejected, verbally assaulting women for rejecting them by ridiculing the women's appearance or using other hurtful tactics. Most of the time women can already sense when they are dealing with a douche and immediately shut things down. It seems as though many men have fragile egos and have ruined the dating scene for *real* men like us. Don't be that guy; don't be the douche.

The way certain men act and perhaps how some of us have acted in the past is the reason why there is distrust and nervousness when men approach women. Past actions have contributed to the bigger communication and trust issue between women and men. As a result of many hurts, disrespect, and insults from men, many women view approaching men with a mixture of attraction or interest, wariness, and trepidation. In a way, women have been conditioned to distrust men on sight. Once again, not their fault! Someone somewhere along the way really messed things up for a lot of us.

The disconnect between men and women comes from a history of rejection and retaliation on both ends. As a result, there is an initial distrust from women as we approach. Have you ever noticed that as you approach or when you spark a conversation with a woman, there are two main types of reactions you will get? Either you will receive a saucy smile with laughing eyes or an indifferent, disinterested perusal. This initial reaction should tell you all about how you should approach, how you should change your approach, or if you should just carry on walking past her and abort the mission.

From the female perspective, a lot can go wrong from the minute you are approaching. A woman might already have her shield going up and mentally be preparing herself to be accosted by another one of the male species. If you do not notice how her body language changes because of these intrusive thoughts, you have probably already gone wrong. It is easy for men to go wrong in their approach because oftentimes you do not know much about the female thought processes and body language yet. Do not worry about that, this book will give you the insight needed! Where you can go wrong includes not listening to a woman's words and actions as well as not thinking past yourself and your desires.

Approaching women in this era requires much thinking, acting, and effective communicative skills. You cannot solely rely on your physique, your beard, your smile, good teeth, or the dimples on either side of your cheeks. This will only get you to the front door, perhaps, even to a meet and greet. Women are able to sense from your manner of speech and choice of wording if you are worth getting to know, a possible fling, or just a waste of their time. Scarily, they can often determine this in under a minute. To create a lasting impression, you have to work hard and take note of the type of woman you are wanting to approach. This book aims to guide you to understand women so that you can assess a successful approach to them and control the events thereafter.

Within this book, you will find helpful tips and steps for understanding what women actually want from a man, how to read their body language so as to guide your communication, how humor tends to make women weak for you, how to use your masculinity as a beacon of attraction, how confidence in yourself makes your attraction level skyrocket, and how having certain communication skills will have her yearning for you. These tools will help you to have the woman of your dreams chasing you down! These techniques will be effective in making you seem more attractive and in leaving behind lasting impressions on the people you interact with. These tools and techniques are essential to building trust in both the talking stage and all the way into marriage. They can even be used in multiple areas of your life when you are aiming to get what you want.

The author of this book has been exactly where you are before. The dating scene is tough, especially when both men and women place so many expectations on the actions of men. Sometimes what everyone is saying will work may not resonate with you and that is because we are all different and innately do things differently. This book will teach you the best ways to go about attracting women while staying true to yourself. Come along and learn all about women and how to get her chasing you!

Chapter 1:

What Women Want

Understanding the Female
Perspective

Men are simpler than you imagine my sweet child. But what goes on in the twisted, tortuous minds of women would baffle anyone. –
Daphne du Maurier

A woman's perspective, mindset and thought processes are quite complicated. Her every action is guided by her feelings and emotions, her environment, her consideration for others, and how people may perceive her. When women choose to go to a shop, they think about where to park, how close their car is to the entrance, which way is best to walk, and if there are any sketchy men around. As soon as a woman sees a man, she is already thinking about all the possible scenarios that could occur with any interaction.

A woman's understanding of the world and herself will affect her every move. To successfully approach a woman, we have to know the ins and outs of the female system! Having knowledge about the female anatomy, psyche, body language, and especially their needs and wants will allow us to get to that desired next level. When you can fully understand the ways of the woman, you will easily have them dancing to your tune! We have to take into consideration that when a woman sees us, they may also see the whole list of previous men who have approached them just as you did!

Women have had to deal with many ups and downs, blunders, systemic oppression, abuse of all kinds, and many disappointments. Unfortunately, this is a result of your gender. Throughout past generations, the male sex has been known to be quite dominating, and not in a sexy way. Often the institutions created by men only serve them, their needs, and their aspirations, while women have had to fight to create their places in these institutions. No wonder they so easily become aggravated by us! For most of their life, men have played a large role in women's unhappiness, disappointment, and sad reality. History is one of the many reasons why approaching women can be unsuccessful, and we may already be at a disadvantage.

This chapter seeks to highlight the perspective of women with regard to the dating field and how this information can be used to men's advantage when trying to woo somebody. The perspective of a woman includes how she perceives men, which will affect how she will perceive and receive you as you make your approach. Knowing what women actually want from men will guide you on how to go about presenting yourself. Women have a very different way of thinking and acting than men. Therefore, understanding the female perspective will guide you on how to communicate with women in all aspects of life.

The relationships between men and women have changed, and the expectations of women vastly differ from that of the 1950s. Women are much more outspoken about their wants, needs, and expectations from men, life, and from themselves. Women are quite independent these days and do many of the activities that men used to solely carry on their shoulders. This includes working long hours, working multiple jobs, working in male-dominated fields, being entrepreneurs, taking their own car to the mechanic, doing DIY projects around the house, and so on. The relationships between men and women are no longer expected to be unequal but have become more of a partnership wherein activities can be shared or properly distributed. In such a partnership, neither one of the partners is put down or carries the burden.

Even though women are capable of doing so many things that men are able to do, that does not mean that she would not want you to do it for her. Women still want a man to take care of certain things that can be seen as very 1950s, excluding the attitude, entitlement, anger issues, and domineering personalities. Some things women may still expect include being the main breadwinner, taking out the garbage, fixing the car, or changing light bulbs. Not every woman wants all of those things, but generally, when men do these activities, they make women feel safe, protected, and provided for. What women want from men is the comfort and the comfortability of having a partner to count on and share activities with. In turn, having a man who feels needed and wanted will make for a pleasant living. I know they say happy wife, happy life but have you ever seen a miserable man? They tend to take everyone down with them!

Women still love it when you open a door for her, let her walk in before you do, pull out a chair for her, and walk on the outside of the pavement. It is all about being thoughtful and making her feel special. Regardless of whether she can and has done many things for herself when she does it all, it all becomes too much, and things may start feeling like a burden to her. Having someone to lighten the load is an exceptional feeling! Be that guy!

As a result of negative reactions from men, a woman's perception of a man as he approaches can differ. Women tend to perceive men as somewhat fragile, and this can determine how they will receive you. The timid but interested reception can be because of curiosity and attraction or fear and placation. From having previous encounters with men with fragile egos, women have regulated their reactions toward men so as to ensure their safety and peace of mind. When you do want to approach a woman, you have to take into account what a woman will see as you make your way over.

Even if a woman is interested in you, she will feel some anxiety as she sees you coming toward her, so it is best not to steamroll on over. When you make an approach, make sure you do not look like you are salivating for her and looking at her as if she is your next conquest. Women like to be approached with a more subtle and humble look, not too egotistical or overconfident. She would like you to smoothly glide over, looking at her in an appreciative manner and with a smile. Sometimes, the women we come across may have a smarter mouth than the rest, but inside, they are all very similar. They are soft-hearted and seek comfort and security. By understanding this simple concept, you will communicate better with women. Food may be the way to a man's heart but being attentive and understanding is the way to a woman's heart!

Knowing what women want from men and life will help to understand what she will want from you! In both physical and online interactions, she wants you to be reliable and present. She would want to be treated as more than an afterthought. Learning the inner workings of a woman will make you more confident in your interactions with the opposite sex. Imagine being able to instantly deflate a situation with a woman before it even escalates. When you understand how to treat and work with any kind of woman, you will be able to move within many different circles.

Grab a note and a pen! Here is a list of things that women want in men. A woman wants a man who is fair, protective, honest, reliable, vulnerable, loyal, displays equality and is assertive. Knowing and acting according to this list will help you become more accustomed to female desires. You should use the above-mentioned tips to schmooze your way into a woman's soft spot!

Key Notes From the Chapter on What Women Want

- A woman's perspective of you will be influenced by her past interactions with men.

- A woman may have anxiety as she sees you approach, so be sure to put her at ease with your charm.

- You will only successfully attract yourself to a woman once you learn to understand her way of thinking and perspective.

- Women seek to have a partnership in which roles, activities, and burdens can be shared.

- Women seek comfort and security. Be the one that can provide that for her.

- Women inherently still want someone to do the manly chores even though they are capable of doing it themselves.

- Fulfilling her needs will inevitably make you feel needed and confident.

- Keep in the back of your mind that women are sensitive and very observant creatures.

- If you act like doing activities for her is the last thing you want to do, expect her to become self-reliant and begin pushing you aside.

Remember that the goal is to have her drawing near to you.

- Women do not like to feel like an afterthought.

- Be considerate of her person, her feelings, and her emotions.

Understanding the perspective of women and their thinking patterns may seem easy on paper and in theory but out in the field, you might still be a bit of a spazz. The following chapter guides you to understand what a woman is thinking or feeling through her body language. A woman's body language is an exact representation of her thought processes as you are speaking or acting toward her. This will incorporate having the background knowledge of what women desire and what they are looking for in you.

Chapter 2:

Listening to Her Body

Language

A Woman's Bodily Cues

They may forget what you said—but they will never forget how you made them feel. –Carl W. Buehner

Communication allows us to communicate our thoughts and perspectives effectively. The way in which we communicate will often have an effect on those around us and can create either a positive or negative reception. What we say and how we express ourselves can easily make conversations go awry. This is something you may have observed when you are speaking to a woman, and you see the smile on her face freeze mid-speech.

Remember when you were younger and playing with your friend on the road. Amid all the laughing and screaming a car horn suddenly blares and you are rushed out of the way. You might not remember all that you were doing but you definitely remember the rush of emotions in that moment. This is similar to how women observe interactions with other people. A woman will remember the way you made her feel in that moment whether it be uncertainty, repulsion, attraction, or comfort. This is why it is important to be aware that how your actions are received by women will leave a lasting impression.

Communication is an essential tool in all aspects of life. The manner in which we speak, our choice of words, and our intonation, all impact the way communication is given and received. We know the drill when it comes to business communication, we know the rules and how to communicate properly. Why do we always make a mess when communicating with women? Perhaps, it is because we do know what is or is not acceptable when communicating with women. As much as it would make interactions easier, unfortunately, women do not come with manuals.

Effective communication skills are really the backbone of lasting relationships. This chapter delves into the verbal and non-verbal ways in which women communicate with each other as well as with you. Certain words and actions will tell you whether or not they are interested or when the conversation wanes. By understanding the way women communicate, you will be able to monitor the conversation by knowing what to do to keep it going and hold her attention. This chapter will guide you on how to read the female body and understand what certain words and actions may indicate.

When approaching a woman, the first thing you should take notice of is her facial expressions. This observation will tell you if your presence is welcomed. Women are expressive creatures and most of the time you will be able to tell how she is feeling nonverbally through either the set of her eyes or her mouth. Sometimes, even in conjunction! Understanding facial expressions can be like reading an emoji; upturned lips are usually welcoming, and a downturned lip is not. When a woman's eyes gleam and are rounded but her mouth is neither turned up or down, take this as a sign of interest but that she is also wary. In such circumstances, your approach should not overwhelm nor intimidate her. Instead, pleasantly walk up to her and try charming techniques such as complimenting her eyes and smile or even humor.

There are many more ways of understanding what a woman is thinking than just from looking at her facial expressions. Some examples of this would be when her eyes are slanted and her lips are slightly upturned, this is often seen as a come-hither look. Just know that if she does this, you are not actually in charge of how the evening is going! If her eyes are slanted or squinted with downturned lips, take this as a sign that you should not even bother. If a woman is not interested at all, simply carry on. Do not take this as a hit to your ego, it could simply mean that she is not in the right mindset to entertain you. Often, as men, we mess up because we are too focused on what we want and not on the other person. Let's try not to make this mistake.

Understanding non-verbal communication is pivotal as most times it precedes verbal communication. Observing from a distance will often guide you on how to interact. Besides facial expressions, you can look at a woman's body to see if you will be received well or when it all starts to go downhill. If a woman is turned toward you, that is taken as a welcoming sign, but if they are slightly turned away, understand that they are not as interested as you are and perhaps, you should bow out. When a woman's hands are rested and her movements are smooth, she is comfortable and receptive to you. Constant fidgeting of the hands is an indication of restlessness. When a woman does this, she would like for you to get to the point, she may be feeling uncomfortable with you or the topic, or she could be pressed for time. Through paying attention to these small yet essential movements you will know when to press onward or when to withdraw in a conversation.

Approaching and physically interacting with women is much different than texting or messaging as here you are able to follow visual cues and sense what to do. This is not true for online platforms and communicating can become more difficult. When texting or messaging you will have to rely on verbal cues sent through text and non-verbal cues if both of you make use of emojis or GIFs. You can tell when a woman is interested based on her reply, this goes for both physical and online interactions. Quick and one-worded replies often tell you that she is not interested and is waiting for you to stop your monologue. Slower and longer replies are an indication that you are asking her deeper questions that require more thought-out answers, and she is taking the time to answer. If she is doing this, she is definitely interested in you and that topic! Quicker replies with a mixture of slow and long answers are an indication of good banter and that she is attracted to you. You are definitely on a winning streak if your conversation flows like that.

Through texting, you will not always be able to gauge the character and personality of whoever you are speaking to. Paying attention to the language as well as the emoticons used will be able to showcase this. Take note of the emojis and gifs she makes use of to understand her interests, the type of media she follows as well as her type of humor. These little details will guide you on how to respond and reciprocate her energy. In the beginning, it is best to follow her lead in the manner of texting. Having a similar manner of texting and banter will allow her to feel more comfortable with you and it will have her seeking you out. Women love to find a kindred spirit as it makes them more expressive, and this tactic will reveal most of what you need to know about her. Her verbal and non-verbal expressions through texts are little bits of information on how she likes to be spoken to, what she likes to speak about, and where her interests lie.

It is important to take notice of when her responses and replies trickle down as this can be an indication that something may have gone wrong on your end. Women are sensitive creatures. In saying that, they can often pick up vibes and can be ruled by their emotions at times. Have you ever noticed that if you are really attracted to a woman, you may tend to text her quite a bit? But suddenly when you are really into the conversation and are sending reply after reply, her responses are no longer as quick! I guarantee that this has happened to many of us, and we simply need to take it as a learning curve. If you come on too strong at the beginning of the texting phase, a woman can feel overwhelmed and slightly put off.

Our responses and replies should always be well-timed as you would want to keep her coming back to you. Responding too quickly may have the above-mentioned effect but responding too slowly will leave her feeling neglected as if you are not that interested in her at all. At the beginning texting phase, you should message her the day after approaching her. Thereafter, message her about twice more within the span of a week. This will have you seeming interested in her but not have you coming across as needy. The best thing to do in the first message after approaching her is to send the "good morning" text. This lets her know that you were thinking about her last night and woke up with her on your mind. Trust me, this thoughtful text often turns women into absolute mush inside!

Women are a lot more sensitive, sensible, and thoughtful than most men. They are much more aware of the softer side of things and often see things from many different perspectives. This has led to them being much more understanding and compassionate than us. That is why it is very important that when we speak or text that we are aware of how we are speaking and what we speak about. There are certain boundaries you should not cross in the beginning—until you know her a little better—and other boundaries you just should not cross at all! In the initial approach and conversation, you should certainly not make any misogynist comments like "smile more," "I like girls who do their make-up like that," "I love it when a woman looks like a woman," or even "you're not like the other girls." If you say these things, immediately her perception of you will change. Women do not always dress or act a certain way to attract men. Often, women are dressing up to feel good about themselves and so that other women will admire their beauty.

Most of the time, when you have crossed a boundary there will be visual cues from a woman. This can include her eyes becoming slitted, mouth pulled tight, a frown, hands being clenched, and her body pulling taught. If she is sitting with her friends, they might share a look of disbelief and confusion at your audacity. Other reactions to you crossing one too many boundaries can include a verbal rebuke or her simply standing up to leave. Take this as your cue to back up and back out, if needed! Similar reactions can be observed through text as well. Women might start to wean you off if you have crossed a boundary or have started to give her the ick! She might start replying less or full-on block you from her social media or contact list.

Understanding and reading a woman's verbal and non-verbal cues will help you to draw her in and keep her wanting more. If you have messed up along the way, you will be able to salvage the conversation by bringing up appropriate and interesting topics once more. Make use of her interests to keep her within reach. Women find it attractive when men are understanding, observant, and attentive! When approaching a woman at this stage, it is all about her. It is about understanding her, her quirks, her interests, and using these observations to create a foundation for your relationship.

Key Notes From the Chapter on Listening to Her Body Language

- Feelings and emotions can be communicated through non-verbal cues.

- Both males and females emit and evoke certain feelings, perspectives, and emotions through their body language.

- Before you approach any woman, it is best to observe her from a distance.

- Never go with your first basic instinct, you will come across as intimidating.

- Be observant. Pay attention to what a woman is saying with her body.

- Use her bodily cues to guide the conversation.

- Make her feel comfortable with you.

- By understanding her body language, you will know when you are contributing too much or too little to the conversation.

- Be careful not to overstep and cross certain boundaries.

- Women are much more sensitive and compassionate than men. Make sure that you do not say anything unpleasant or make any insensitive comments.

- Watch her facial expression to see if she is smiling and enjoying your presence or if she keeps looking away for help.

- Her body language will tell you whether she is comfortable or not.

- Idle hands and an open chest indicate that she is enjoying your company.

- Avoid misogynistic comments.

- Do not compliment her on her physical appearance right off the bat.

- If you do want to flatter her, make mention of her smile, her eyes, or her fashion sense.

- Avoid sexual innuendos at all costs!

Being observant, attentive, and carving out time to understand women will benefit you in the long run. Knowing what boundaries not to cross is essential in allowing a woman to feel safe and comfortable with you. This is further discussed in the next chapter where you will be guided on how to draw her in deeper using charisma!

Chapter 3:

Humor Feeds the Soul

Why Laughter Is the Best Medicine

A person without a sense of humor is like a wagon without springs. It's jolted by every pebble on the road. –Henry Ward Beecher

Laughter is the best medicine in all areas of communication! It is a way to ease tension, it is used as icebreakers, and to get the crowd going. There are many benefits to laughing such as releasing stress, bringing people together, and uplifting someone when they are down. Laughter is simply a gift, and it is a gift that opens up many avenues when trying to get to know someone.

Someone with good humor is always attractive to women. If you have been saving some jokes, then this is your sign to try them on a woman you are interested in! This area can be a little tricky though. Do not be that guy who simply walks up to a gorgeous woman and immediately starts cracking jokes. This could paint you as the weird guy who will live on as a cringe-worthy topic of conversation between that woman and her girlfriends. Trust me, you will be known as that weirdo from the bar for years to come!

Knowing when to joke and what to joke about plays a pivotal role in how a woman will look at you. This chapter aims to guide you on how to go about introducing humor into the conversation as well as which themes of humor are appropriate. It will discuss why humor plays such a great role in attraction and how you can use this to your advantage. Her body language and reception of a joke will often tell whether you are treading on thin ice or should simply disappear! Humor is important to females in a partner and this chapter will show you how to go about it all.

Having a sense of humor is peak attraction to women! Some jokes, ribbing, and teasing a smile out of a woman has gotten me out of a few ill-thought-out situations. Often, women can be blinded by a pretty smile, a deep laugh, and a good sense of humor. If this is up your alley and if you are a goofy guy, then you should definitely use this as both your choice of weapon and armor. Humor easily puts someone at ease, and it will allow a woman to feel more comfortable with you.

What is even better than good humor, you may ask? The answer is having great banter! Flirting is the art of small talk. It includes a lot of playfulness, smooth conversation skills, and high social intelligence. In fact, with the right words, tonality, and right "approach," you can make anything highly attractive (Asher, 2020). Creating and having good and flirtatious banter without crossing boundaries will have her feeling your vibe.

Remember women are very intuitive and if she finds a kindred spirit in you, she will actively pursue you.

In the long run, having a partner who is light-hearted and funny will help relationships in many ways. Especially when times seem dark, it is always best to have someone who will let a few sunrays spill through. Finding humor in and with each other will help create a foundation in which both of you can explore each other's goofy side and act naturally with each other. Starting a relationship with pretenses, this includes both the conversation and the texting stage, leads to distrust and nastiness. Throwing yourself into the deep end with a sense of humor is definitely the way to go but let's not do it in an obnoxious way. Be cool and smooth with it.

When you smile at a woman in appreciation and not in a lustful or overly sexualized manner, it will get you the sweetest, most precious reaction. This is a reaction you truly want. The way women respond to a beautiful smile and *good* humor is downright magnificent. When you show appreciation in a respectable way, women will often respond better. Women have been around a lot of poorly mannered men so when you approach them in this manner, you will have already created a lasting impression as well as sparked interest on her end. Once you get her smiling back at you, take that as your directive to approach. The name of the game is now to keep her smiling!

Although laughter is always good, the things we joke about and what we laugh at may vastly differ from what women will laugh at. We need to take into account what topics and themes are appropriate when approaching a woman. Almost 80% of the jokes you make with your male friends are off-limits! Save that for much later in the relationship. You will be able to tell whether or not your humor is welcome when the responses start waning and she no longer giggles or laughs. These are often the type of women who are not as confrontational but beware of the ones that are! They will tear into and seriously educate you on how disgusting and inappropriate your joke was in their opinion, and kudos to them. As men, we have been conditioned to speak and act however we want, and many times we have gone unchecked.

To properly associate and converse with women, we have to know what the boundaries of good humor are and how certain jokes can ride roughshod right over them. To successfully introduce humor into the conversation, it is always best to be politically correct, socially aware, and sensitive. We live in an environment where people are easily triggered, so it is important that we think about what humor is appropriate. Because women are more socially adept and conscious, the first date or conversation should really not involve any political or socio-cultural humor. Unless, of course, she is the one to introduce those themes. The topic of conversation and humor may also be affected by your surrounding environment. The best thing to do in these circumstances is to simply follow her lead!

There are certain themes of humor that we have to be aware of, not use until we are all comfortable with each other and better understand each other's personalities. There is a thin line between dark humor and crossing the boundary. Jokes that are uncultured, uncouth, involve disabilities and disparities, are down-right mean, or are crude, are a serious no-no in the beginning. Pay attention to the topics she brings forth and her tone of voice. This can imply her feelings toward the topic, and this is something you should take note of. Look for openings in her language use that may indicate sarcasm or wit and use this as your cue to find some humor. Once again, pay close attention to her and use this to guide your conversation!

In the previous chapter, we explored body language, and this can play a major role in the reception of your sense of humor. You will be able to sense if she is attracted to you and your humor by the way she is laughing. A woman's type of laughter can range from a grin or giggle all the way to a throaty or whistling laugh! A grin or giggle is often an indication of wary interest as if she is still checking you out. On the other hand, boisterous laughter, Mariah Carey whistling notes, and snorts are an indication that you both have similar humor and that she is absolutely loving it. Either that or alcohol has entered the chat! This gradient scale may tell you if you are on the right path.

To make sure that you do not cross the boundaries and put a woman off, there are certain topics of jokes that are appropriate. First off, a few knock-knock jokes are always welcome. They are safe and super cheesy, but they will always garner a light laugh here and there. You can take your cues from any humorous comments she makes as well. You can definitely make jokes at your own expense. This will draw on women's sympathetic nature in which they may contradict you and try to make you feel better. You can use this to your advantage to turn the situation around and flirt with her. Flirtatious banter is a great way to keep things going and it will have her giggling constantly.

Before you approach a woman, it is always best to sit back and observe. Observe how she interacts within her environment and with her friends. Let's not try to approach a woman who we can clearly see is not in the mood or does not seem to have many similarities to you as an individual. Remember, just because she is attractive does not necessarily mean you are attracted to her. Let's not waste anybody's time here! It is important to know the type of woman you want and the type of woman you will be approaching.

Laughter and humor are great tools of attraction to use in both physical and online interactions. Making use of jokes in physical interactions is easy and natural as the banter may be livelier as opposed to texting. In physical interactions, humor is used in verbal forms, facial expressions, and gesticulation. On the other hand, when texting you will mostly rely on text, emojis, GIFs, and even voice notes to relay humor. Humor can come through with the use of silly emojis and laughing gifs in texts. You can also use uppercase letters to show excitement as well as change the font to bold or italics to showcase the mood behind your text. As you may not know each other just yet, these methods and tools of communicating humor are to showcase your own humor and personality.

Key Notes From the Chapter on Humor Feeds the Soul

- Use laughter as an icebreaker and to get her feeling comfortable with you.

- Women find humor very attractive.

- Do not be obnoxious with the jokes. This is not the time to be the class clown.

- Good humor can get you out of some tough spots!

- Women seek humorous partners who will make her laugh when they are stressed or feeling down.

- Avoid mean or crude jokes.

- Avoid controversial topics.

- Use her choice of topics as a guide for the direction of the conversation.

- Take note of any sarcasm or irony she might use. These are indicators of what she might find humorous.

- Use her type of laughter as an indication of how attractive she finds you.

- If her laugh is quite boisterous, she is attracted to you.

- If her grin is strained or lopsided, she probably would like for it all to end soon.

- If you run out of jokes, use yourself as the butt of the joke. This could have her sympathizing with you and stroking your ego. If she does this, she is probably interested in you.

- Do not make insensitive jokes.

- In online interactions, use emojis and gifs to show humor and emotion.

- Too much use of laughing phases can actually irritate a woman as this may have her viewing you as someone who does not take things seriously.

- Create a space in which you can be humorous together.

- The aim of the game is to have similar humor and laugh at things together, Jokes should not be one-sided.

Laughter is essential to any sort of relationship foundation. With women being sensitive and thoughtful creatures, having a partner who takes note of that is extremely attractive. What is even more attractive is when they share similar humorous anecdotes and are able to feed off of each other's happy vibes. Insensitivity is a major turn-off! As men, we can be quite insensitive at times. Some see it as a marker for masculinity and virility but essentially it is simply selfish and mean. The following chapter delves into the connotation of masculinity and how to make it work for us.

Chapter 4:

Masculinity

How to Become More Self-Aware

Being a male is a matter of birth. Being a man is a matter of choice. –Edwin Louis Cole

Have you ever seen how babies run away from their own shadows? Frankly, it's hilarious. Sometimes women can have the same reaction to seeing men. Shadows are often large and imposing. When we see our shadows all we see is an intrusive, dominating outline and darkness. Many women view men in this way as well.

When women see men approaching, they do not look at the features or clothing that you are wearing. Their brains immediately register your large size and imposing figure. They can be daunted by the appearance of men, so it is important that we not come across as overly aggressive, imposing, or scary. Especially because most women are smaller than us.

Even though we might find pride in our masculinity, our appearance can be quite daunting to women who have been intimidated by other men. We have seen this countless times as we walk outside alone, often women will choose to walk on the opposite side of the street. When we see a woman walking alone to her car and a truck or van is parked next to her, immediately she will be alert and wary. This is a result of the era we are currently living in, in which women have to constantly watch their backs and watch out for each other because of the depravities committed by other men. In the dating field, when approaching a woman, and texting her we have to be aware of how we may come across. Will we be perceived as intimidating and scary, or can we use our size to provide feelings of safety and protection?

The female perspective is guided and jaded by their environment and their past encounters with other men. Unfortunately, few men take the time to understand females and their perceptions of reality. Usually, they just go about their day and talk to women however they want. As a result of many men going unchecked, they walk around with arrogance and way too much confidence in themselves. When these kinds of men approach women, they leave lasting negative impressions of all men. It is hard to not generalize men and toxic masculinity from a woman's perspective if the majority of the men that she encounters purely suck!

From the female perspective, masculinity is observed very differently than from the male perspective. Many females have been victims of poor manners and attitudes from men. Men can be domineering and intimidating, and often, use these traits as a means to bully someone into obligation or submission.

Sometimes men can be so obnoxious that they even wear women down and coerce them into doing things.

Being *that* guy can come across as being obnoxious and a nuisance. There are a lot of lost people out there who want to be "the guy." The guy that walks into the room and instantly commands attention. The guy who meets women effortlessly (Powers, 2013). However, often being that guy will get you into a lot of trouble and women will not want to give you any time and attention. Masculinity does not necessarily mean you have to act according to the macho male stereotypes to get the hot girl. There are many roads that lead to the same destination.

Learning to use our masculinity in a different, more comforting manner is the key to attracting women to us. This chapter highlights the highs and lows of being masculine in an era where it might not be as welcoming. This chapter will delve into the types of masculine features that women really appreciate and crave. It will guide you on how to use those masculine sides to successfully attract the woman you want and how to keep her waiting for more. The tools acquired from reading this chapter are also a guide on how to speak and act with women even outside of attraction.

There is more than one way of observing masculinity in this day and age. Masculine used to only refer to giant, hairy, tree-trunk toting men. Survivalists and mountaineers, if you will, but this is no longer the case. A man can be masculine because of height, brawn, and size or simply because of certain actions which show him to be the light of a provider and caretaker. Masculinity has been annexed due to so many men being a poor representation of what it means to be masculine. These types of men can include the gym bros, douches, men with frat boy mentalities, and overly possessive or dominant men. There seems to be a great divide in masculinity because of the men who have toxic masculine traits who have fooled many women versus those who are way more laid back and honest. This is probably why many of us good guys are still struggling in the dating scene.

There are both advantages and disadvantages to being masculine. Not all masculine traits are physical. Some traits go much deeper than your appearance. Many times, the most masculine burly-looking men showcase none of the more important masculine traits behind closed doors such as taking care of things in the house or supporting their partner. On the other hand, some men who might not look as buffed up are the ones making the most effort and who have the deeper masculine attributes. These men make time to take care of and support their partners.

Physical masculinity can be advantageous as some women find larger men very attractive. However, they are let down once they notice that a lot of men only have their physique going for them. Some men are found lacking in the character department and despite being attractive on the outside, they can come across as selfish and self-absorbed. This is when masculinity can be disadvantageous and has also contributed to the perception that if a man looks too masculine, he is probably not too smart, he likes to play the field, or he probably makes misogynistic comments. We have always heard the phrase "nice guys finish last" but in truth, the nice guys have the longest lasting and healthiest relationships. The best way to make your masculinity work for you is to play on the needs that women want men to take care of.

Beware of misogynistic and chauvinistic behavior and commentary. These types of behavior will immediately have a woman running away. Women take the first instance of poor behavior as an indicator that it might not get any better. Therefore, any male superiority or male dominant behavior will easily have the conversation going awry. Mean and stubborn behavior is unappealing and unattractive to women because it shows that you could be difficult and disappointing down the road. In order to attract yourself to her, make sure that your behavior is the total opposite of this.

Your size, build, and stature can work to your advantage! Women love to feel petite, protected, and cozy. Regardless, if the men are these things for their women, having a man who shrouds her with his size can be a serious turn-on but only if you have worked hard to create a space in which she is safe and comfortable. I think we already know that in other events as well, size does matter! Using your masculinity in a protective nature will have you achieving major attractive points. Even women who you are not seeking to attract will be drawn to you simply because you move in a manner that is masculine but does not make them fearful.

Size and manner play a pivotal role in the reception of men by women. Larger can mean more threatening and overpowering which can scare away certain petite women. On the other hand, many women still find this size attractive even if they are slightly intimidated. Leaner men may not be as threatening, but at times they can be grouped with party people, soccer players, or other groups that may have a negative reputation. Relying on the physical aspects of masculinity is not always a win-win situation. Therefore, it is best to play on character and actions to woo a woman. The more gentlemanly activities you do for her, the more masculine you will appear to her. Regardless of size and physique, manners are where it's at!

Your size and manner can be used to your advantage. If you are a larger man, it is important that you not look like your girth is a struggle. Women like suave and sophisticated men. Let your walk be graceful and confident. If you are a man with a leaner build it is important that you not come across as unconfident and withdrawn. Use your build to appear less imposing and friendlier. Women cannot resist returning a charming, friendly, and kind smile.

As men, we can definitely use our attractive physical features to attract women but if that is all we have to offer, things can go downhill from there pretty quickly! That is why it is important to work on good character traits. Another way in which you can use your masculinity to your advantage is to adopt traditional masculine roles. Traditional masculine roles include taking care of household needs and protecting one's family. If women still like to feel cherished, protected and cared for, then this is definitely your way in. Playing on the emotional needs of women will have her wanting and needing you around. Thoughtful and gentlemanly behavior is one way to surely keep her attraction to you growing.

Using what a woman wants, needs, or expects of you to your advantage might seem wrong to some. Isn't that being manipulative (Louis and Copeland, 2009), you may ask. To some, it may seem to be a manipulation technique, but it can only be so if you are not being true to yourself and your feelings at that very moment. The word manipulation has had a bad reputation because so many have used it for their own personal gain and amusement. Technically, to manipulate refers to being skillful. Using such skills to make sure a woman feels safe, comfortable, and heard or to endear her to you with the best intentions cannot be so wrong, can it?

Masculinity can serve as a major attraction point in physical interactions when you display thoughtful behavior and mannerisms. Such as being attentive, making sure she is comfortable, asking her where she would like to go next and being patient with her. When a woman notices that you are taking time to make sure she feels good and that you seem like a good person, she will want to see you again! In text form, masculinity will come through in different ways. When chatting with her, you will have to be attentive and present. This will have her feeling appreciative toward you and wanting to reciprocate. When you make her feel good, this is a sure way to have her chasing you!

Self-awareness as a man comes into play in all aspects of communicating with women. We have to be aware of the impact that masculinity has had on the female perspective and generational thinking as well. Being self-aware will benefit both the way you view yourself and how the woman you are approaching will view you. If you condition yourself to appeal less threateningly and more openly, you will definitely attract more women! When women view you as less of a threat and as an equal, she will feel comfortable exploring more with you.

Femicide, woman abuse, and female intimidation is not anything new. In a world where women are much more vocal about injustices, there seems to have been a rise in abuse and assault cases. These dangers are always at the back of a woman's mind whenever she is approached by a man who has an imposing figure or who is quite dominant. Toxic masculinity has played a major role in warping the perception of what it actually means to be a man. In saying this, when you interact with a woman it is always best to make sure that she feels at ease!

Being self-aware of your masculinity and how it comes across will affect the way in which a woman receives you and if she will want to see you again. Be aware of the way you speak, act, and touch a woman. Make sure that you do not cross certain boundaries such as being too forward in the places you touch her. too much physical affection without checking in on her comfort level can be off-putting and place her on the defense. Be subtle and make use of gentlemanly behavior. This will feed her attraction to you as she feels safe and sees something in you that has not been witnessed in past encounters with men.

It is best to avoid making commentary about her body size and shape. Women have created a body positivity movement which celebrates and accepts all women's bodies and why they are made a certain way. Do not start commenting on how voluptuous or slender she is! As much as women love to be complimented and to know that you find her desirable, she would like to be treated as a normal person, too. If you come at her physical appearance right off of the bat, she will assume you only want one thing from her. We all know what that is, don't we?

Key Notes From the Chapter on Masculinity

- Masculinity can be both advantageous and a disadvantage.

- Understand how toxic masculinity has affected how females perceive men.

- Be aware of your own faulty traits that may contribute to how men are perceived.

- Size and aggressive mannerisms may intimidate women.

- Be aware that how you act around or address women may leave them feeling anxious and uncomfortable.

- Understand how femicide and gender-based violence play a role in how a woman might receive you.

- Masculinity is not so much in your physique but more in your actions.

- What makes a man is their character and actions.

- Being a gentleman is still secretly a trait coveted by women.

- Try to be less intimidating and imposing.

- Do not put a woman on the defense. Usually, there is no recovering from that.

- A woman would still like for you to take care of and provide certain things for her.

- Masculine features such as height, girth, facial hair, or large hands are found attractive by women, but these attractions may fade if all you bring to the table is good features.

- Play up your character and personality.

- Good character and personality leave lasting impressions and will have you constantly on her mind.

- If men have treated her badly in the past, then you treating her spectacularly will have her coming after you.

- Avoid overly aggressive maneuvers such as touching her without her permission.

- Avoid mansplaining and talking over her in conversations.

- Use your masculinity to feed her physical and emotional needs.

- Be considerate and patient with her.

Making use of positive mannerisms associated with masculinity and using it to nurture certain aspects in women will have her feeling cherished. Regardless of whether you appear extremely masculine or not, it is more about character and personality traits than muscles. In the end this is what women find most attractive in the long run. The next chapter delves into how women find men who are simply themselves—and have good, relatable personalities—very attractive.

Chapter 5:

Just Be Yourself

Why Acting Natural Is Beneficial

I promise you there are also women out there who just want to experience another person, have a connection, bring meaning to their lives by exploring life with someone who gets them. –RenÉe Carlino

I am sure we have all stopped and stared at the sky after a storm or as the sun sets. We look at the finite details and are stunned by the natural beauty of it all. If we find so much beauty in natural movements, how is it that we do our best not to be our natural selves around women? Sometimes, men can be quite harsh on themselves. Most men hide lots of insecurities and do not view themselves as beautiful. It is time to pull up your socks and see yourself the way others do!

Have we not wondered at natural things in all their beauty? I am pretty sure we have all stopped and stared at an attractive woman as she walked past us. Her natural movements, the swaying of her hips, the unbothered smile, her hair bouncing in the wind, and the twinkle in her eyes. It is simply fascinating when you see a beautiful creature in her element, hypnotizing men as she walks on by. This must surely be how the pirates of old in those fictional dramas felt when they came across a siren at the shore! Men view women as naturally feminine beings who are confident and seductive without even trying.

Even though we perceive women to be as such, we often do not observe ourselves in the same manner, do we? Men try so hard to conform to the standards of other men and the rules set out by the majority of men in order to attract the female we want. This sheep mentality is probably what led to "toxic masculinity" in the first place. This chapter will discuss how to rid you of those preconceived notions on how you must act in order to get the girl you want. This chapter aims to give you tips and guidelines on how to be comfortable with who you are and how being yourself will work to your advantage!

Both women and men have fallen prey to dates who have put on a front. Oftentimes, we follow the rules or examples set by our friends and our environment and use them as a set of guidelines when talking to women. These rules include aggressively placing yourself in a woman's personal space, whistling at a female you find appealing, and giving her a sly smile while eyeing her assets. Most of the time they are absolutely rubbish! These rules were used and set by men who love to play the field when it comes to women. These tools and mechanisms used by men have contributed to the "*love-em and leave-em*" mentality that many women have fallen victim to. Putting on a front and being anything but who you truly are will only lead to disaster!

The way we act with our friends and how we act around a woman can vastly differ. I know you act more raucous and sillier in a comfortable environment with friends as opposed to in the company of someone you are attracted to. If you and your friends have a crude and hilariously mean way of speaking to each other, it might be best to keep that side of you at bay. However, this does not mean that you should totally have a different personality when you are with someone you are attracted to. Sooner or later the real you will pop out of the closet and who knows what will happen then. If there is a reason you are hiding your true self away, you might have a bigger problem on your hands.

Acting natural, goofy, and messy can be seen as peak attraction to most women. A woman secretly craves someone they can be natural and goofy with. If you show up and are natural with a woman from the get-go, this will allow her to feel just as natural and comfortable with you. Having this foundation of comfortability and honesty early on in a relationship will lead to the ability to be open and honest with each other regarding many other topics. Who wouldn't want to be around someone with whom they can truly be themselves around?

In this society, people are judged for every little thing. It might be a little difficult these days to just be a man because the world is jaded by the acts of so many other men. You also have to deal with generational ideology on what it means to be a man. Sometimes it can be a little hard to be ourselves when we are afraid of how everyone else will look at us. Not fully being able to be yourself and become who we truly want to be can greatly affect our confidence. This, in turn, can negatively affect the way that women perceive us.

Women may perceive unconfident men as unattractive! If you look as if the world is on your shoulders or that life has beaten you down, how can you possibly seem attractive to someone? If women are looking to men for a partnership, having someone to talk to and to put their trust in, you have to look like the man that can do it all. Unfortunately, unconfident and pathetic-looking men can give women the ick when they are on the prowl! Confidence in your skills, your person, and your capabilities will draw women toward you.

Confidence will make you seem more attractive because to a woman it will seem as if you are capable of doing many things. You will be perceived as someone they can trust and come to with their problems. Women will see your confidence as an indicator that you know what you want, and you know how to go after it. Having confidence in yourself will garner you major attractive points!

When you are confident, it will attract a certain type of woman. If you are confident in your fashion sense, you will attract a woman who appreciates that and is able to bond with you over that. The law of attraction is essentially that you will be attracted to someone that you share similarities and interests with. By being confident in yourself and your quirks, you will attract someone whose personality complements yours. Being confident in yourself and knowing who you are will allow you to attract the person who will truly appreciate you. Having confidence will boost your appeal and attraction to everyone around you! It will even affect more than your personal or romantic life.

Acting natural and being confident can have many benefits. It will help you to seem more approachable to both women and businesses. In fact, it can open up all kinds of avenues for you. Acting natural when approaching a woman will immediately put her at ease with your presence and have her divulging her interests in no time at all. By being natural upfront with her, you will be creating a safe space that will actually help you get to the good part much sooner. Definitely much sooner than people who tend to put up fronts or who are not as confident. Inconsistencies in your character will cause doubts! Women are very observant and intuitive so if you are not being true to yourself in that moment, her Spidey senses will definitely be tingling!

When you are true to yourself, it shows her that you are unafraid and confident with her and your life. Beware of the fine line between being comfortable with yourself and showing that to others versus being unapologetically yourself. The latter often leaves you looking obnoxious and selfish. This will not attract anyone, let alone a woman. "Being yourself" doesn't mean that you are utterly impulsive and driven by whatever behavior is most convenient for you in the moment" (Louis and Copeland, 2009). Here is where being yourself and toxic masculinity can overlap. Avoid being this guy at all costs. Being yourself entails being natural and at peace with your true self and not trying to be someone else.

Being confident and natural in both physical and online interactions can come through in the way you walk, talk, and gesture. Having ill confidence and insecurities are judged much harsher in men as opposed to women. So, unfortunately, if you come across as having too many insecurities or not enough confidence, a woman will either be sympathetic to you, or she will be turned away! Indecisiveness is looked upon poorly. If you are not confident in choosing your drink, how can she possibly trust you to have confidence in making major decisions? If you fail to be confident in many things, perhaps, you are not really ready for the pressure of taking a woman out for the evening.

Your confidence and being natural can come across in different ways through text. How you are naturally can come through the way you speak, the types of topics you speak about, and the type of humor you have. If she responds well to these and reciprocates your energy, just know that you have allowed her to feel the same and she is comfortable being as natural with you as you are with her. In online interactions, confidence will come across in making plans or stating your opinions. Having an opinion is very different from something such as mansplaining. Especially if your opinion does not belittle or chastise her opinions on the topic.

There is a fine line between being confident and arrogant. Here you might find yourself crossing over to be overconfident and obnoxious. No one likes a know-it-all, so overconfidence will have you losing major attraction points. It is off-putting to women when you are arrogant and overbearing when you approach or talk to her. This was explored in Chapter 3 when not being self-aware can contribute to your detriment. Sometimes overconfidence can ruin it all!

Recently, the topic of mansplaining has come up. If you are unfamiliar with what mansplaining is, it is basically the event in which men feel the need to unnecessarily give their opinion and explanation on things that do not really have anything to do with them. In fact, most of the time your explanation will be incorrect and uneducated. If you find yourself in these circumstances, I beg of you to just keep quiet. Arrogance and ego play a huge part in mansplaining, and it contributes to the negative way in which women perceive us. This is why communication plays such an important role between men and women.

Key Notes From the Chapter on Just Be Yourself

- Women love a man who is comfortable being himself around them.

- Do not try to hide your true nature or put on a front.

- Women want someone who they can be natural and silly around.

- Create a space where both of you are able to be true to yourself around each other. This will lay a foundation for trust and open communication.

- Be confident in yourself.

- Women perceive ill confidence as unattractive in men.

- If you do not have confidence in yourself, she will not have any confidence in anything you bring to the table.

- Learn to be confident in all areas of your life. This will affect the way people perceive you and how you perceive your environment.

- Having confidence will boost your self-esteem.

- Be confident, not overly confident or arrogant.

- Arrogance can lead to egotistical behavior which will affect the way you treat a woman.

- Be humble. Humility will endear her to you.

- Women want a man to listen to them.

- Being yourself allows for a safe space in which opinions and perspectives can be shared.

- Create a space in which a woman feels safe and comfortable, a space in which she can freely express herself.

- When a woman feels this way, she will not want to leave anytime soon! In fact, she will make sure to keep it that way.

Sometimes women simply want you to listen to them. Not be overbearing or arrogant in your explanations. Knowing how to communicate with women will help you to get to where you need to be. The next chapter will guide you on how to properly talk to women in a way that will have them coming back for more!

Chapter 6:

Communication Is Key

Why Broken Communication Is at the Root of Failure

Much unhappiness has come into the world because of bewilderment and things left unsaid. –Fyodor Dostoevsky

Communication can make or break a relationship. It is important that you hear what a woman says and try to communicate your thoughts and opinions in a manner that is not hurtful. The key to good communication is allowing one another to express ourselves and an environment that is not judgmental.

Many things go unsaid and unheard which can affect how we treat one another. Proper communication skills are a key component to most successes in life. Broken communication is at the heart of many failed partnerships and relationships. When you do not hear what the other person is saying or refuse to see their point of view, communication starts to fail. Having good communication skills is essential when talking to women. Women place high value in men when they actively try to communicate with them in a manner that is thoughtful and kind. The ability to talk your way around people will have them eating out of the palm of your hand!

Have you ever been to a flea market and suddenly many vendors are vying for your attention? When you visit one stall, suddenly the vendor is trying to sell you more than what you are looking for. Somehow you end up paying for much more than you initially planned. Mind-boggled, you walk away wondering how it all went so wrong! These guys are professionals when it comes to knowing how to get what they want through sly communication maneuvers.

Communication can seriously go awry when we misspeak or do not consider the repercussions of how the things we say may be received. This is especially true when we speak to a woman. Have you ever been slapped by a woman or had a woman walk away from you, leaving you behind wondering where it all went wrong. You probably said something really insensitive. Like in the earlier chapters, knowing how to properly communicate incorporates understanding females and being aware of your own downfalls.

If you know how to treat and speak to women, you will have them coming back for more of your considerate acts. Communication is the key to your success in having women chasing you. When she has been treated abhorrently by other men, the way you treat her and speak to her will be refreshing. This will have her thinking that being with you might be worth the long game. Like the vendors that were mentioned before, effective communication skills will have her wanting more.

Good communication can create a solid foundation in a relationship, but miscommunication will have that foundation crumbling. Just like the childhood game, Broken Telephone, when someone mishears or misspeaks, a lot of things can go wrong. This chapter will discuss how broken communication can lead to doubt and dissatisfaction in relationships and between men and women. It delves into how men sometimes fail to communicate properly and thus, self-sabotage. This chapter serves as a guideline for how to effectively communicate with women.

Countless women have been victims of the player mentality of men in the dating scene. This may be where your initial approach to a woman may go wrong. As you approach and start speaking with her, your words may start to sound way too familiar to her. Is it simply déjà vu or are you using text from the player handbook on how to get the girl? she has probably heard it all before and that may skew her perception of anything further you have to say. Approaching her with all the sleazy confidence of a man who has been around the block will damper communication on both ends!

I am guessing that you have chosen to read or buy this book because the player handbook has probably not worked out. You have probably seen that it does not yield lasting results and perhaps, you want something more substantial. If you have chosen it for these reasons, then congratulate yourself on actually becoming a man! Women seek mature thinking and acting men who can communicate properly. This does not mean being serious all the time, we have already discussed how women enjoy having a humorous partner. It simply means that they want someone they can trust to talk to about all sorts of things and receive supportive feedback.

How to communicate properly includes listening to her and answering her in a manner that does not shame or hurt her. Having good communication allows for everyone to express themselves honestly and not be afraid of rebuke. It is a safe space where you can also express your innermost thoughts and have a supporting shoulder. Proper communication skills take into consideration the speaker and the receiver's environment, state of mind, emotions, and background. Effective communication consists of thinking about someone else's feelings before your own and thinking about the best possible answer.

Good communication includes understanding a woman's communication, verbal, and non-verbal cues. This will guide you on when to act and when to stop speaking. When a woman notices that you take time to consider her feelings, emotions, and opinions before speaking, she will view you as a catch. Cue the accumulating attraction points! Good communication is all about consideration. If you take time before you respond and carefully word your answers, she will appreciate you all the more.

Good communication is also about reciprocation. A relationship cannot be one-sided with one person being the aggressor. You cannot simply ask all the questions about her, even if you want to know all that there is to her. Keep that excitement at bay. If she notices that you keep pressing her for answers, but you barely answer her questions, she might become a little suspicious! You have to be open with your communication, your ideas, as well as feelings and perspectives. When there is open and forthright communication between you both, this will allow for a space of trust. If a woman finds herself trusting you, she will want to share more of herself with you.

We have previously discussed how a woman's bodily cues communicate how she is feeling. Sometimes, men do not realize just how powerful they can communicate with their own body language as well. You might not realize how strong the vibrations you put out may be, how it comes across to a woman, and how she understands it. That is why knowing how to speak to a woman and express ourselves correctly is important in growing attraction. This includes playing no games with her emotions and being vulnerable and accessible to a woman.

If you communicate well, it will make her attraction to you grow because she will start to feel as if you are making her a priority. If and when you make a woman feel special, she will want to come around more often. The aim is to make her stick around so you can show her that you are different from the other men she has been around because you talk to her as if she matters. Good communication skills are super attractive to women because not all men actually listen to them. Giving them that platform and spotlight makes them feel the same to speak with you on many topics. If she feels safe with you, then you have passed through the front door and made it into the heart of the home!

There are many ways to keep a woman interested in you through proper communication. Most of it involves listening to her and being attentive. If you constantly ask a woman her opinion and input on topics and decisions, she will feel as if her opinion matters to you. Thus, she will start to feel as if *she* matters to you. The key to using communication to feed attraction is to make a woman feel as if you consider her in all your actions. Have you told a woman that you will drive by her apartment later but failed to specify a time? Being considerate is an important area in good communication. Next time tell her you will specify a time or tell her when you are leaving the house. If the drive is taking a little longer than usual due to you making a few pit stops along the way, make sure to let her know so that she is not left feeling stranded.

Here is where things can become tricky. A woman wants you to be attentive but not overwhelming and clingy! Asking her opinions and input is all well and dandy until you ask her about every little pesky detail. Communicating where you are going and what you are doing is to placate each other and let them know that you are safe and sound. When you start being overbearing, wanting to know where she is going, who she is with, and wanting to know her every move, this is when communication can start breaking down. The same can happen from a man's point of view if he is constantly being questioned about his whereabouts, it can lay a foundation of mistrust! Having mistrust between two people can affect all aspects of communication so it is imperative that there is honesty between you all right from the beginning!

Men have been known to still chat to and entertain other women in the beginning stages. Do not make this mistake. If you are attracted to a woman and would like things to go further, I suggest that you cut off all other romantic situations with the previous women in your life. Things can become disastrous for you if a woman finds out that you are simply wasting her time! If a woman has been burned one too many times before, she will definitely take the first sign of infidelity and distrust as her cue to fly like a bat out of hell! Just like the "good morning" text which shows appreciation and consideration to the woman you are attracted to, there are many ways to communicate with her that she is special to you. If a woman feels like she is your everything and that you make her a priority, she is bound to do the same for you.

We have previously mentioned that you should text the woman you are attracted to and chasing, about twice within the first week of meeting, but what happens after that? Here you really have to be careful. You cannot push too much or give her too much time in between hearing from you. You can actually chat with her twice a week for about the first month. Consistency is key but after that first month, she might start squirming in her seat. This is when you take it up a notch and start making plans to see her if you have not done so already.

Communication includes more than just the verbal aspect. To show a woman that you are a good communicator, you have to physically show up as well. Knowing that she can rely on your word is great but when she realizes that she can depend on you to physically be there, just know that she plans to stick close to you. Activate God status! Make it a priority to physically see her within a month of approaching her! Once she sees that you are there and so much different than the poor excuse of men she is used to, you bet she will want you around longer and will put in as much effort into the relationship as it needs. Soon she will start making plans with you, wanting you to meet her friends, and she will have you accompanying her to events.

An effective way to highlight that you are willing to meet her halfway or to show her that you are making an effort is to pay attention to her Love Language. This is a tool used in many relationships as communicating in more than one way is essential to wooing a woman. Her Love Language may be physical touch, quality time, words of affirmation, acts of service, or receiving gifts. If you nurture these aspects and speak to her through her love language, she will bloom before your eyes, and so will the relationship. Knowing your Love Language and making your partner aware of it is just as important. A relationship in which both parties' needs are met will lead to better communication and overall relationship.

Key Notes From the Chapter on Communication

- Broken communication leads to a poor foundation on relationships.

- Use good communication to create an area of trust and honesty.

- Proper communication skills can be used to control and turn conversations around.

- Skillful communicators can easily diffuse situations.

- Be open and honest with her.

- Try to understand her point of view.

- Do not speak to her in a manner that makes her feel unintelligent.

- Show her that her opinion matters to you.

- Always express yourself verbally. Do not let anger or frustration build up.

- Talk things over as soon as there is a difference of opinions.

- Do not leave matters left unsaid and unresolved.

- Do not communicate with other females.

- Be consistent in your communication.

- Ask her about her daily life and show her that you are interested in all aspects of her.

- Communication includes both verbal and non-verbal communication.

- Be present in both your texts and actions.

- Let her know about your whereabouts. Involve her in *your* daily life.

- Do not ghost her. A woman wants someone she can rely on.

- Communication can fail when you let your insecurities override rationality.

- Do not overwhelm her and suffocate her with questions about her whereabouts.

- If you do not trust each other, this will come through in how you communicate with one another.

- Get to know her Love Language and nurture those areas to appeal to her.

- Making her a priority will have her wanting to stick around.

- When she observes that you are taking your time to understand and talk to her, she will make sure to keep you around.

Communication is an accumulation of all of the previously mentioned guidelines and tools. It incorporates understanding women, knowing how to read her body language, knowing how to put a smile on her face, understanding how your masculinity can affect how you communicate, how the way in which you communicate will be perceived by a woman, and how confidence affects relationships. All these factors work together to help you get the girl!

Conclusion

How to Get the Girl Chasing You

I wanted to drown inside a woman in the feeling and drooling of the love I could give her. I wanted her pulse to crush me with its intensity. That's what I wanted. —Zusak

As much as there is an emphasis on women wanting security and a solid relationship, many of us guys want that too! Perhaps, it is too soft and unmanly to say that aloud but deep down we know it is true. In order to truly have the women chasing us, we have to be prepared to feel vulnerable.

What is the end goal of reading this book? Is it love, is it a partnership, or are we simply lonely? If it is the latter, kindly skedaddle! Approaching a woman, preparing for a date, and wanting to start a relationship requires us to know what our end goal is. You should be here because you are serious about finding a life partner, truly understanding women, and wanting more than casual flings. This book has detailed essential tools on how to get a woman seriously attracted to you. To get to this peak attractive status, there are many things you need to learn, adapt to, and adopt.

There can be many complications from both the male and the female perspective which can hinder a relationship. This can play a role from the minute you approach or even look at her. Both of you come to the table with your own frame of reference, perceptions of reality, and all sorts of baggage which can affect how you perceive each other. A woman's perspective is affected by the actions of other men. As well as guidelines and warnings from female predecessors told through the generations on how men will do you wrong. In contrast, men are taught by their male predecessors about how to treat women. Most of the time these lessons are more about male preservation, self-esteem, and feeding your own needs! All of these notions can affect the way we talk and act.

Both men and women have difficulties in the dating scene. Sometimes, it can be hard to garner attention, attraction, and keep someone attracted to you. The major things that can affect you in the dating scene are areas of self-confidence. Knowing your worth and how people perceive you can work to your advantage. If you know exactly how to work the people around you, you will always be able to get your desired effects! Think of the world as a game of chess and yourself as the player. Understanding the roles and mechanisms in a game of chess, knowing how to maneuver each pawn in order to get the king which serves as the prize. Each of the chapter titles such as understanding a woman's perspective, using her body language to guide your actions, having a good sense of humor, understanding the powers of masculinity, being confident in yourself, and effective communication serves to make you aware of certain roles, actions, and qualities that you can use to get women to find you attractive.

Knowing who you are and what you want in a partner or out of life is essential when going out into the world. Most women take the time to understand themselves, their bodies, and where they have gone wrong. Sometimes, they may take a whole different approach! I am sure that after being rejected many times, only then did you decide that something may be wrong on your end. Women are much more intuitive than you. In fact, many women have taken the time to know their Love Language, and I suggest you do the same. Knowing each other's love language will guide you on how to better treat each other! If her Love Language is affection, then using that language is how you should approach her to stay in her favor.

Each of the titles discussed and the application of the above steps changes the game. The implementation of these actions serves to influence the innermost workings and thought processes of women. By knowing and using these important steps meant to endear women toward you, in no time at all will she be the one chasing you. Women enjoy it when men make the first move and keep coming back, showing them that you are interested in them. By constantly showing up and letting her know that you are extremely attracted to her and that you would like to see where the relationship can go, she will become just as excited to be with you. Women love consistency. If she sees that you are actively trying to stay around, she will soon be actively making sure to keep you around.

Understanding the female mindset, being yourself, being self-aware, having good character, having great humor, putting her at ease, being considerate, being a good listener, and being attentive, will aid in your success! These are core changes that will make a difference in the way you view yourself and the way women will view you. By playing up on these components, you will have her chasing you. These qualities and meeting men who have almost all of them are few and far between! Once she sees that you are a great package, she will actively do things to keep you around. Oh, how the tables will turn!

Being honest with yourself and being true to your nature will get you further in the dating scene and relationships than being what you think women would want. Scrap all of your preconceived notions on how to attract women by being *that* guy! Essentially you should not have to change who you are to fit into the social constructs and systems regarding dating and relationships. You do not have to look a certain way to attract someone. The real trick is in knowing how to talk with her and make her feel special.

The purpose of this book is to have the woman you are attracted to start chasing you. These guidelines show different angles that may come to you naturally or those which you need to acquire. Unfortunately, there are many things men have to unlearn in order to treat women better. To get the girl chasing you, inevitably you have to show her a range of behaviors that paint you in a positive light. As soon as she sees that you display behavior and manners unlike she has been shown before—and that you treat her as if she is the apple of your eye—she will put in much more effort to make sure you do not leave or stray!

If she enjoys your company and the type of man you are, she will be chasing you. Women are looking for someone they can trust, be themselves with, relax and unwind with, and someone who shows them stability. If she sees that you have these basics, she is all yours! Make use of these guidelines and tools to have her coming back for more of you. If you really want her to start chasing, make her feel as if she does not want to lose you.

eferences

Asher, R. (2020). *How to flirt with women: The art of flirting without being creepy that turns her on!* How to approach, talk to and attract women (Dating advice for men). Viebooks LLC.

Carlino, R. (2019). *The last post.* Atria books.

Cole, E. L. (1982). *Maximized Manhood.* Whitaker Distribution.

Du Maurier, D. (2003). *Rebecca.* Hachette Digital.

Evans, R. L. (1971). *Richard Evans' quote book.* Publishers Press.

Louis, R and Copeland, D. (2009). *How to talk to women.* Prentice Hall Press.

Powers, T. (2013). How to talk to women: Unlock the secrets to effective attraction, flirting and girlfriend getting. Velocity House.

Quarantine memories daily notes. (2020). *Quarantine Memories Notebook With Unique Touch.* Independently published.

Sapp, S. E. (2019). *Staying the Course: A Guide of Best Practices for School Leaders.* Rowman & Littlefield.

Zusak, M. (2004). *Getting the girl (Wol*